HOW TO
QUIETEN
YOUR MIND

ANNA
BARNES

CONTENTS

INTRODUCTION

Life is so busy nowadays, whether
you're rushed off your feet at
school, college or work, or your
family or social life is full to the
brim. There is so much to do, so
many things to organise and so
many people to see. With being
busy comes noise, and an awful
lot of mental chatter. If your mind
is constantly running it can be
distracting, especially if – like many
people – your thoughts are filled
with worries or anxieties. A noisy
mind can dim the bright flame of
who you truly are. But peace is
within your reach: this book will
show you how to listen to the
thoughts you're having, and help
you to separate the helpful from
unhelpful ones to get your inner
monologue to hush up a little.

When you arise in
the morning, think of
what a precious privilege it
is to be alive – to breathe,
to think, to enjoy, to love.

Marcus Aurelius

A LITTLE BIT
OF QUIETNESS
EVERY DAY

PRACTISE GRATITUDE

Take a few quiet minutes to think of everything in life that you are grateful for, and spend some time appreciating the simple things you may be taking for granted. Be thankful for the roof over your head, for having food in your cupboards and a warm bed at night, and for your morning cup of tea. Take a new perspective on those things that we so often forget to be thankful for, and cherish the feeling of sunshine on your face, having water to drink or the luxury of a hot shower. Perhaps you have a pet that brings you comfort and joy or a close family that you love. Write a list of the things you are grateful for in a notebook that can be kept in easy reach. When you're feeling low, open it up and read it. Reminding yourself how blessed you are can help ease a mind filled with worry.

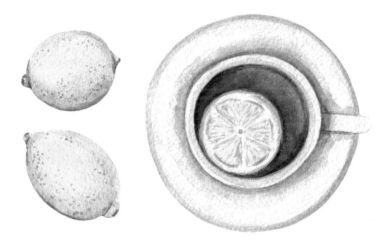

I GET THOSE FLEETING, BEAUTIFUL MOMENTS OF INNER PEACE AND STILLNESS

– AND THEN THE OTHER 23 HOURS AND 45 MINUTES OF THE DAY, I'M A HUMAN TRYING TO MAKE IT THROUGH IN THIS WORLD.

Ellen DeGeneres on meditation

Dedicating a small amount of time per day to worry about the things that are bothering you has been proven to make the worry seem smaller. Set aside ten minutes in your day specifically to let your mind worry about a problem and look for a solution, and spend the rest of the day worry-free.

GO QUIETLY

Soak in as much silence as you can
in the day. Resist the temptation to
put in your headphones or have some
form of background noise as you go
about your life. Encourage peace and
tranquillity, and follow in their example.

Not everything has to be done in a day, especially if you risk doing a task to a standard you won't be happy with. Reassess when essential tasks need to be done by, and prioritise your to-do list. Can something you've been trying to cram into your week be done at the weekend, or could you spread a big task out over several days to keep you refreshed and your mind focused?

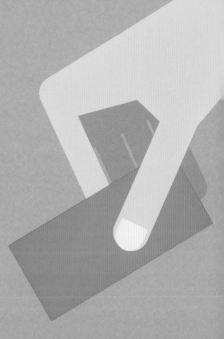

REMAIN CALM, SERENE, ALWAYS IN CONTROL OF YOURSELF. YOU WILL THEN FIND OUT

HOW EASY IT IS TO GET ALONG.

Paramahansa Yogananda

GET TO SLEEP

When you are ready to turn in, make sure your bedroom is as dark as you can get it. Turn off all lights, cover the glare from any electronics you have, and if you own an electronic alarm clock, change the settings in the display to get the light that shows the time as dim as possible. Once you're in bed and all warm, allow your mind to wander, but don't pay attention to the chatter. Instead, focus on your heartbeat and your breathing, and try to slow them down if you feel anxious or panic-stricken. If your thoughts are too intrusive to allow this, try redirecting your mind and thinking about what you would like to dream about, and focusing on pleasant thoughts instead. It may take a few nights to perfect the skill, but your mind will catch on.

UNPLUG

Have a technology-free day.
Step away from your gadgets, and
spend a day going back to basics
by putting your creative skills
into action with a 'studio day'.

While away the hours drawing,
painting, or simply cutting and
sticking. Your mind will benefit
from the quietness that comes
without the constant stimuli
from phones and computers.

PEACE AND SERENITY

ARE

WITHIN YOUR GRASP

EMBRACE STILLNESS

Just sit still. Do it for a minute
at first, then two, then three.
Do it each day until you can
manage to have ten minutes
in complete peace. During this
time, focus on whatever you
like, or nothing at all, and enjoy
the mental calm it brings.

THE EARTH HAS MUSIC FOR THOSE WHO LISTEN.

George Santayana

SING!

Sing a happy song at the top of your voice. In private or public – it doesn't matter. Dance along, and focus on the lyrics you're belting out. If you do it in the morning after getting up, it will set the mood for the day.

LET NATURE WORK ITS MAGIC

Spending time in the great outdoors
lifts your spirits. It has also been
proven that 'forest bathing', or
spending some time amongst trees
on a regular basis, can lower your
heart rate and blood pressure,
reduce stress, boost your immune
system, increase focus and energy,

and help improve your quality of
sleep. What's more, this magical
form of therapy is free. So take time
whenever you can to get outside
and be at one with nature, and let
it work its healing powers on you.
A stroll in the outdoors will do
you a world of good and give your
mind time to work out problems.

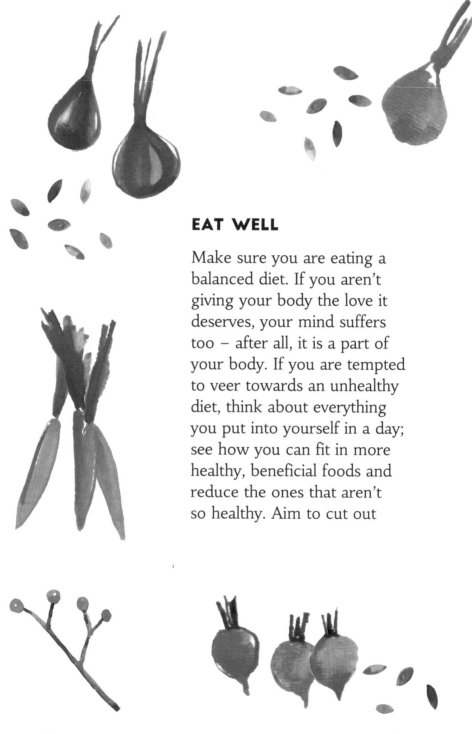

EAT WELL

Make sure you are eating a balanced diet. If you aren't giving your body the love it deserves, your mind suffers too – after all, it is a part of your body. If you are tempted to veer towards an unhealthy diet, think about everything you put into yourself in a day; see how you can fit in more healthy, beneficial foods and reduce the ones that aren't so healthy. Aim to cut out

the processed, sugary meals and drinks, and refuel with fruits, vegetables and legumes instead. If you eat meat, cut back on your consumption, or change the way it's prepared – there's no health benefit to fried chicken! The effects won't take long to be noticed; you'll feel brighter, more refreshed and energetic, and have a renewed passion and drive for the world about you.

MAKE A MEAL OF IT

Spending time making a healthy and fulfilling breakfast, lunch or dinner can help you focus your mind and is something that will benefit you entirely. There's nothing better than eating a delicious, healthy meal with the satisfaction of having made it all by yourself.

SAVOUR
MEALTIMES

Take your time when it comes
to mealtimes. Don't rush them; they
are important times of the day.
Treat each meal as a ritual, where
you give yourself time to relax and
enjoy the activity. Take a meditative
approach, where you eat slowly,
savouring the flavours of
each mouthful.

eating well is a form of self-respect

A QUIET HOME

ADJUST YOUR MINDSET

Acknowledge where you are right now, and set your brain to the appropriate mode. If you're at home, you should feel relaxed. If you're at the gym, you should feel energised. If you're at work, you should feel productive and focused. Take a moment to get into the right mindset before you go about your day.

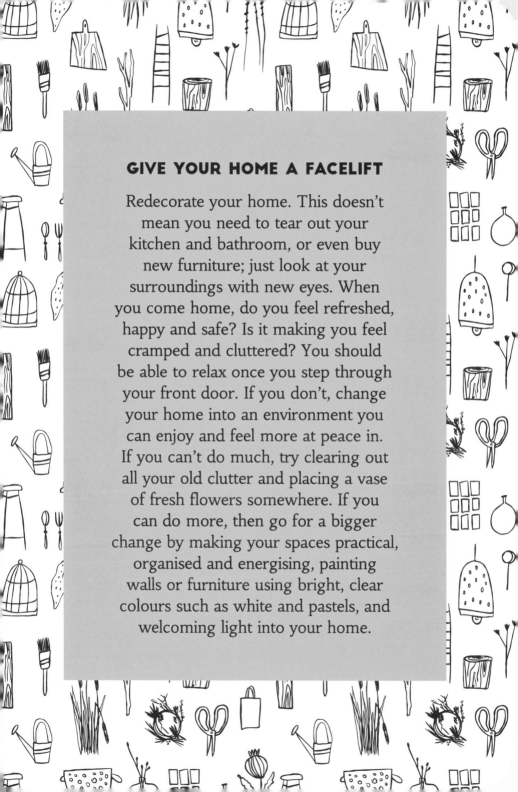

GIVE YOUR HOME A FACELIFT

Redecorate your home. This doesn't mean you need to tear out your kitchen and bathroom, or even buy new furniture; just look at your surroundings with new eyes. When you come home, do you feel refreshed, happy and safe? Is it making you feel cramped and cluttered? You should be able to relax once you step through your front door. If you don't, change your home into an environment you can enjoy and feel more at peace in. If you can't do much, try clearing out all your old clutter and placing a vase of fresh flowers somewhere. If you can do more, then go for a bigger change by making your spaces practical, organised and energising, painting walls or furniture using bright, clear colours such as white and pastels, and welcoming light into your home.

The best and most beautiful things in the world cannot be seen or even touched; they must be felt with the heart.

Helen Keller

PLAY GAMES

Play a board game or video game with friends. Your mind will enjoy focusing on challenges that bring instant rewards, and spending quality time sharing a new activity with friends means you'll come away refreshed.

AFFIRMATIONS

Write down some empowering affirmations or your favourite positive quotes, and stick them up around your home in places you're likely to see them often, such as on the bathroom mirror or on the door of the fridge. Repeat their words to yourself every time you see them or whenever you feel your mind racing, so that you can bring your thoughts back to their calm, powerful meanings. Try picking some of your favourites from this book, or from your favourite novels.

Silence

is

luxury

TURN THAT FROWN
UPSIDE DOWN

Find somewhere quiet when
you get home where you
can lie on the floor and place
your legs up against a wall for
ten or fifteen minutes. This
is particularly helpful if you
spend all day sitting down.
Let your body relax, and allow
the increased blood flow to
your brain relieve it of excess
thoughts and refresh your
whole body after a long day.

YOUR SACRED SPACE IS WHERE YOU CAN FIND YOURSELF OVER AND OVER AGAIN.

Joseph Campbell

MAKE LIGHT WORK OF CHORES

Household chores need to be completed, but they aren't particularly fun. Sometimes we send our thoughts into a panic because we start thinking about all the things that need doing: cleaning the bathroom, the kitchen, vacuuming, doing the laundry, doing the washing up... But why not try breaking these things down and taking small steps every day, rather than letting it all build up, so it's never one huge, daunting task?

For instance, keep a bottle of anti-bacterial spray and a couple of clean cloths in the bathroom and wipe down surfaces every couple of days. Then, the prospect of 'cleaning the bathroom' won't seem so bad because you've already done part of the task. Simplify your routines, and look for 'chore cheats' you can use to free up your time for the fun stuff.

ENJOY ALONE TIME

Learn to love being alone with
yourself and try not to fill every
waking moment distracting
yourself from your own company.
Spend some time alone regularly
– perhaps you could treat yourself
to dinner, or a film, or go for a
relaxing stroll around the park.
It could even just be an evening
in with your favourite show.
You're great company if you'd
just give yourself a chance.

YOU ARE CONSTANTLY
CREATING YOURSELF

HAVE A RELAXING BATH OR SHOWER

Take the time to spoil yourself
next time you wash: do all
those things you might delegate
to 'just for special occasions'.
Light some scented candles
or dim the lighting, and put
on some relaxing music.
Use a bath bomb or special
shower gel and a face mask,
and scrub all the parts of you
that might go neglected. Take
your time, appreciating the
warmth of the water on your
skin and letting your muscles
soak and relax, and reconnect
with your body once again.

A silence with you is not a silence, but a moment rich with peace.

Leonard Nimoy

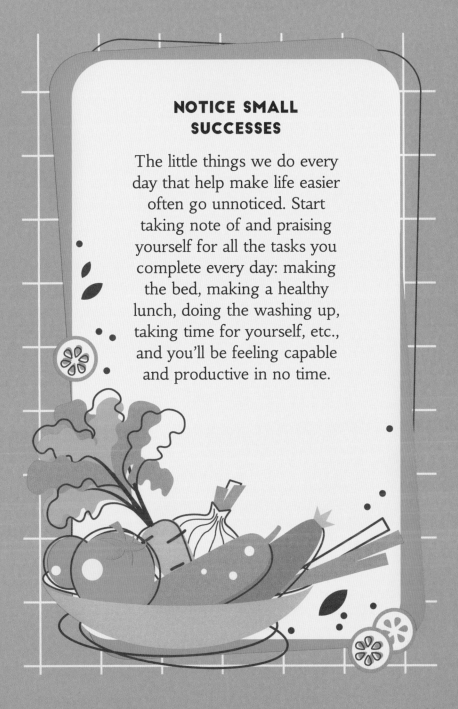

NOTICE SMALL SUCCESSES

The little things we do every day that help make life easier often go unnoticed. Start taking note of and praising yourself for all the tasks you complete every day: making the bed, making a healthy lunch, doing the washing up, taking time for yourself, etc., and you'll be feeling capable and productive in no time.

Our
greatest
experiences
are our
quiet
moments.

Friedrich Nietzsche

calmness

COMES WITH

Rest

MAKE YOUR BEDROOM
A SLEEP SANCTUARY

Take a few moments to consider your usual bedtime routine; what time do you normally go to bed, how do you feel when you're in your bedroom and what else do you do in there? Make sure you're heading to bed at a sensible time: getting the recommended eight hours of sleep can work wonders for you, so if you're due to wake at 7 a.m., going to bed past midnight isn't the best for your health. If you struggle to fall asleep at night, it could be because you associate your bedroom with other activities. Try leaving all your electronics in another room, having an alarm clock instead of relying on your phone to wake you up and starting a night-time routine to get yourself into a sleepy mindset.

Your bedroom should have you feeling relaxed and calm the moment you set foot in it. Make your bedroom a sleep-only area, cleanse it of all other influences and redirect them to other parts of your home. You'll dream better in no time.

CALM IS A SUPERPOWER

QUIETER
EMOTIONS

KNOW YOUR WORTH

We all feel stress or discontent when we feel like our efforts are being undervalued, so take a moment to think about and acknowledge all the things you do for other people. If you feel like you've been taking on too much, it's perfectly acceptable to take a step back – saying no to those extra tasks at work, or to babysitting for a friend when you don't really have the time, can help alleviate your stress and prevent the feeling that your kindness is being taken for granted. If you are happy with your workload but feel your inputs aren't being appreciated, speak to your boss about how you feel – perhaps going for a pay rise or promotion would make you feel more content?

HAVE A SOCIAL-MEDIA CLEANSE

If you're on a social media platform,
think about what you're using it for.
Spend some time unfollowing accounts
that don't leave you feeling good, and
look for positive accounts you could
follow that spread inspiration, positivity
and joy. Check your privacy settings
to see if you can free your newsfeeds
from unnecessary influences and
advertising, and prioritise the people
and accounts that make you feel great.

HAVE A DIGITAL CLEANSE

Uninstall all those apps you don't use or that don't bring you joy, turn off all but essential notifications and reflect on what information you're gaining from these tools. Don't overwhelm yourself with unnecessary news or updates from friends – stick to the things that actually benefit you.

Whatever makes you happy,

do that

LOCK UP YOUR WORRIES

Find a wooden box or a mason
jar. Whenever you're feeling
overwhelmed, write down all your
stresses, concerns or worries on
scraps of paper and put them into
the box. By writing down what
troubles you, you can help to ease
the burden you feel, and by doing
this, a lot of issues won't seem
so big any more. When you put
those problem thoughts into the
box, try to really feel as if you are
giving those troubles away – they
don't belong to you anymore.
Don't open the box other than to
add new worries to it. Know that
you have trapped all the negative
thoughts in a small space away
from you, so your mind can feel
it has been freed of worries.

DETOX YOUR SOCIAL LIFE

Cut out negative influences in
your life. If there is someone
that causes you to feel a lot of
negative emotions and their
presence doesn't bring you
joy, reassess their value in your
life. If that negative energy
can be removed, take action,
and don't feel bad about it.
You deserve happiness.

NO ONE CAN MAKE YOU FEEL INFERIOR WITHOUT YOUR CONSENT.

Eleanor Roosevelt

FOCUS ON WHAT
YOU CAN CONTROL

There is so much that is uncertain, but
there are also many things you can change
if you put your energy into them. If you're
feeling at a loss, find something productive
and healthy that you can channel your
energy into, such as yoga or art or learning
a new language. That way you'll be safe
in the knowledge that this is an area of
life you have total control over, and it
can be a source of happiness and calm.

BELIEVE THAT GOOD THINGS ARE COMING

GIVE YOURSELF A BREAK

Take rests when you notice your
productivity is flagging. There is
no point in forcing yourself to do
something when you're not focused
on it. Instead, it causes anxiety and
invites your brain to come up with
ways to avoid the task altogether.
In order to be healthy and productive,
your body and mind need time to
recharge, so step away and come
back to it later when you're
feeling more energised.

MAKE THE MOST OF
YOUR PRODUCTIVITY

When you get a burst of energy and
are feeling productive, find ways to
get as much done as possible. Make
a list of all the things you want to
achieve, cut out all distractions, make
sure you have some healthy snacks and
water to hand to keep you hydrated,
then get going. Afterwards you can
enjoy the feeling that you have made
progress, and know you have earnt
some down-time as a reward.

IF YOU GET TIRED, LEARN TO REST, NOT TO QUIT.

Banksy

KNOW HOW
TO DELEGATE

If you're overwhelmed with
tasks, delegate things to other
people. Even if you feel like
you don't have authority, don't
be afraid to ask if someone
can do you a small favour
– it's always OK to ask for
help. Just be sure to return
the action when you have a
chance, and everyone wins.

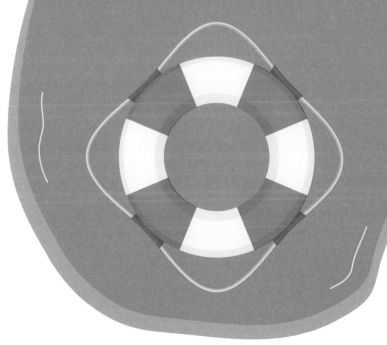

TURN YOUR PROBLEMS
INTO POSSIBILITIES

It is easy to view something that has not gone to plan as a problem. However, that's closing the door on all the opportunities that may have come up as a result. For example, if you applied for your dream job and you didn't get it, instead of giving up and feeling rejected, think of all the other options you now have! You could look into taking a gap year, try your hand at a totally new career that you've always been interested in, or learn from the process and use it to prepare for other job applications that will undoubtedly come up in the future. Just because something you want didn't happen this time, it doesn't mean you can't still get it. Perhaps the timing wasn't right, or the path you are taking might have a few more twists and turns than expected, but if you keep an open mind, even things that seem like failures at the time might lead you in exciting and unexpected directions.

You are

tranquillity

YOU ARE ENOUGH

Know that you are enough, for this moment in time, for your friends and family, and the world around you. You owe no one an explanation for your existence. You are allowed to do and feel as you please.

REFRESH YOUR ATTENTION SPAN

Modern-day life means lots of us are constantly checking our phones for texts or emails or scrolling through our social-media feeds. This ruins our attention span, making big tasks seem more daunting, and causes anxiety when we don't get our social-media 'hit'. To return your attention span to its natural level, try reading a book for ten minutes without checking an electronic device, then twenty minutes the next day, building up until you can spend an hour reading without the urge to constantly check your phone. A refreshed attention span means a quieter, more productive mind.

Be the silent watcher of your thoughts and behaviour. You are beneath the thinker. You are the stillness beneath the mental noise. You are the love and joy beneath the pain.

Eckhart Tolle

DON'T LEAP TO CONCLUSIONS

Don't assign meanings to everything
that happens to you in life. Sometimes,
things just happen. Sometimes, other
people just don't think about their
actions – they are often too wrapped
up in their own challenges to notice
how they might have affected you.
If you feel affronted by a friend, for
example, take a step back from the
situation and have a look at it again.

Is it possible you have put too much thought into something they said or did? If you still think they were at fault, speak to your friend about how it made you feel and put your mind at ease. Otherwise, give them the benefit of the doubt and assume they meant no harm – after all, most people are just going about their daily lives with no intention of hurting or offending others, especially their friends.

Become grounded
and at one with
the world

FIND SOMETHING YOU LOVE

If you haven't found your passion yet, go searching for it. Look for classes in your local area online, or try signing up for a new experience that you think you might enjoy. Once you find something that makes your heart happy, embrace it wholeheartedly.

I never lose sight of the fact that just being is fun.

Katharine Hepburn

LEARN NEW SKILLS

An overactive mind might be your brain's way of
telling you it wants more stimulation. Try learning a
new language or learning how to play an instrument
to give it something new and exciting to focus on
and distract it from its usual routines of worrying.
Intellectually stimulate yourself more, and your mind
will re-engage with the more important things in life.

STOP PROCRASTINATING!

So much of the mental noise in our heads comes from worrying about the things on our to-do lists. The feeling of not wanting to do a task is often worse than actually doing it. Steer your mind away from fretting, and break up the dreaded tasks into tiny, bite-sized chunks that you know you can achieve with ease. Count down from five all the way to one to steel yourself, and then just start. If you manage just one of the bite-sized chunks, it will relieve a bit of your stress and remind you how capable you are. You might find it so satisfying that you want to carry on and do another chunk, or you may even be able to do the whole thing in one go when it's broken up into less daunting sections. Bite the bullet and get that task done, so you can tick it off your list and give your mind some peace.

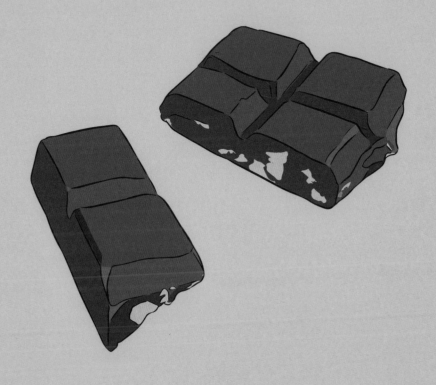

TO BE QUIET OF MIND IS A CHOICE

5
4
3
2
1
0

THE FIVE-SECOND RULE

Allow yourself a five-second stress-out. Count backwards from five, allowing your thoughts to race and go where they will, but once you hit zero, move on from whatever it was that was causing you distress. The countdown tricks your mind into thinking it's getting its own way, and helps release those anxious thoughts that have been building up, and then allows you to get on with your day.

DON'T AIM FOR PERFECTION

You don't always have to do everything perfectly, look perfect or be the perfect employee/family member/friend. No one else is perfect (if it looks like they are, it's probably a clever mirage), so why should you be? Take the pressure off by accepting that mistakes happen, and can be resolved, and that getting things done is what matters – not achieving absolute perfection in every task. So sack off the ironing once in a while and embrace that creased shirt, knowing that your mind is thanking you for giving it a break.

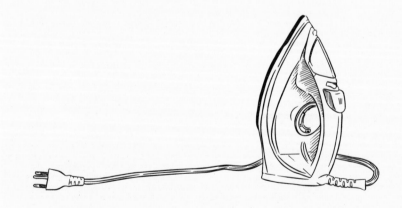

THE POWER
OF THE MIND

LOOK FOR THE POSITIVE SIDE

We're all guilty of it at times, but moaning
and making a fuss about situations that
are out of your control only serve to make
you more tense and stressed, as well as
making those around you stressed too!
If you can do something about it, do. If
you can't, try to look for the positives in
the situation. Ask yourself: will I still be
annoyed about this situation tomorrow,
or next week, or next year? Or will I find
it funny? When something goes wrong,
take a brief moment to acknowledge what
has happened and then, if you can, laugh
about it. When you decide to search for
the lighter moments in the things that
cause you stress, you are better able to
control the situation by properly processing
what has happened, and you can react
in a calmer, much more productive
manner. You can then move on, safe in
the knowledge the situation is dealt with
and you haven't wasted valuable time
on something that was unavoidable.

Radiate
love and
happiness

MAKE POSITIVE CHANGES

If you're unsatisfied with your current situation,
there's nearly always something you can do to
change it – even if you think you're powerless
or fighting a losing battle. Take action to
start changing the negatives into positives –
find those little ways you can make yourself
happy, and create a positive environment.

A SENSE OF CALM

If you're panicking due to all the
things going on in your mind,
distract yourself with your senses.
What can you see right now? What
can you smell? What can you
feel? What can you hear? What
can you taste? Your mind will be
pulled into the present moment,
and the events around you.

SET PEACE OF MIND AS YOUR HIGHEST GOAL,

AND ORGANISE YOUR LIFE AROUND IT.

Brian Tracy

THROW OUT UNLIKELY SCENARIOS

So you're having negative thoughts about something you think might happen. Think things through logically and carefully. How likely is this scenario to happen in real life? If you have lots of evidence for it happening, then prepare yourself practically as best you can, but if not, toss out the thought with a laugh. Don't entertain scary scenarios for no benefit to yourself.

worrying does not create peace

PRACTISE MINDFULNESS

Reminding yourself how to be in the moment and acknowledge what is happening around you will stop your thoughts from straying into unhelpful territory and can help your mind from racing ahead in panic. For an instant dose of mindfulness try stopping whatever you're doing right now and assess how you feel inside and out right in this very moment. Alternatively, try slowing an action you do regularly right down – maybe it's preparing a meal, or brushing your teeth – and really paying attention to every motion. Look for a class or app to help you incorporate mindfulness into your daily life.

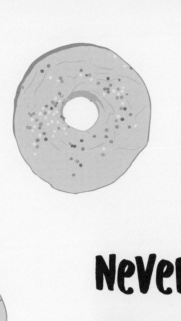

NEVER FEEL GUILTY FOR WANTING WHAT YOU WANT

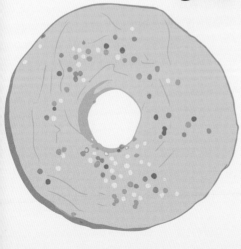

SEPARATE YOUR NEEDS
FROM YOUR WANTS

Falling into the trap of mistaking our wants
for our needs can make us feel unsatisfied
and distressed. When you experience strong
cravings for something, take a second to
think about how you're feeling at that
moment in time – what is your body telling
you you need? If, for example, you'd really
like a slice of cake, think about whether
this might be because you're hungry and
that is the first bit of food you can see,
or because you are craving a sugar fix?
Then think logically: your body might
need food, but it does not need cake.

Do what's right for your body: try drinking
a large glass of water and see if you still feel
hungry afterwards. If so, give it something
nutritious like a piece of fruit or a handful
of nuts and the craving is likely to go
away. Sometimes, our wants and needs
overlap, and can seem like the same thing.
It is important to learn to identify which is
which. When you start to pay attention to
and satisfy your needs, you will discover
a more peaceful mind is inevitable, as
you are not searching to quieten it with
things you do not ultimately desire.

SAY NO

No is a powerful word. Don't
be afraid to use it when you feel
pressured to do something you're
not comfortable with. It doesn't
matter what it is; if you're unhappy,
stressed or uncomfortable, say no.

SAY YES!

The word yes can open up doors we didn't expect to find, like a new friend, new job or new experience. Say yes to going for lunch with a co-worker you don't usually socialise with, or yes to trying new food or new activities; you never know what great things could happen.

Quiet people
have the
loudest minds.

Stephen Hawking

TALK TO YOUR
OVERLY ACTIVE MIND

It may seem silly at first, but
your mind may just be trying to
remind you of something that
needs to be done, or something
you've forgotten. Talk to it,
and listen to what it's trying
to tell you. Once your worries
have been acknowledged,
they are free to drift away.

WRITE DOWN YOUR WORRIES

Think through the catastrophic scenarios your mind likes to think up. Write them down to get them physically out of your head, or share them with others – whether talking them through on the phone, in person or in the form of a letter. Suddenly, the scenarios won't seem so realistic or so scary.

CREATE A SURVIVAL PLAN

There are very few genuine end-of-the-world events, but for the few that do exist, there are plans in place for dealing with them. If you are worrying about something that you feel could actually happen to you, create a realistic survival plan. Don't let yourself be caught up in the 'what ifs'. Think through a viable solution that you'll have to hand should the worst actually happen.

WHAT WE THINK, *we* become.

Buddhist proverb

FIND YOUR POSITIVE VOICE

Think about the voice inside your head, and every time it decides to say something unhelpful, negative or unnecessary, change that voice. Make it the voice of someone that you find easy to fight back against – perhaps it's a small, pathetic voice that you can easily ignore or see in a silly light. Then in a clear, authoritative tone, calmly tell that first voice to go away, and follow it up with some positive affirmations to drown out the 'bad' voice. Then assign all the helpful, positive thoughts to this 'good', confident voice (maybe this positive voice sounds like a more self-assured version of your own, or of that of someone you love). Soon, you won't hear the bad thoughts, just those from the good voice; after all, who needs to listen to those negative thoughts when you have such a powerful, strong and positive voice to stand up to them?

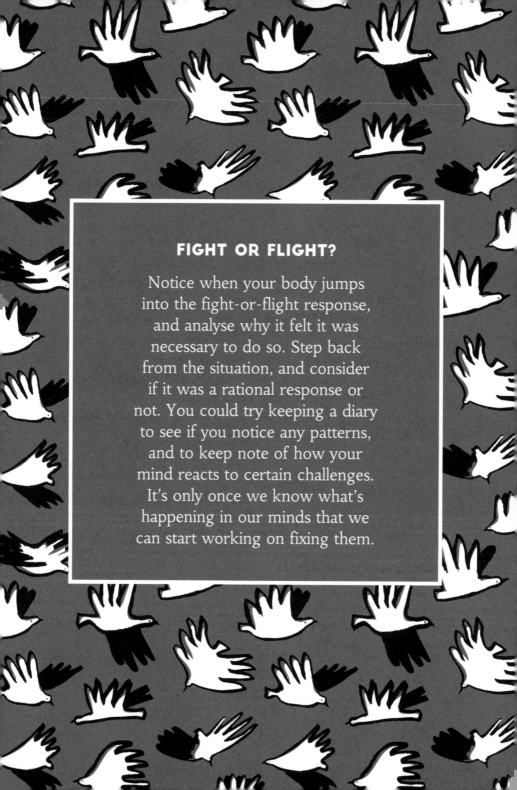

FIGHT OR FLIGHT?

Notice when your body jumps into the fight-or-flight response, and analyse why it felt it was necessary to do so. Step back from the situation, and consider if it was a rational response or not. You could try keeping a diary to see if you notice any patterns, and to keep note of how your mind reacts to certain challenges. It's only once we know what's happening in our minds that we can start working on fixing them.

POSITIVE THINKING

You don't need to focus on negative
outcomes. So what if something
bad has happened? Don't let it
spoil your day. Acknowledge the
situation, then shrug, laugh and
move on. There's little to be gained
from dwelling on negativity.

Have
AN
INCREDIBLE,
calm
LIFE

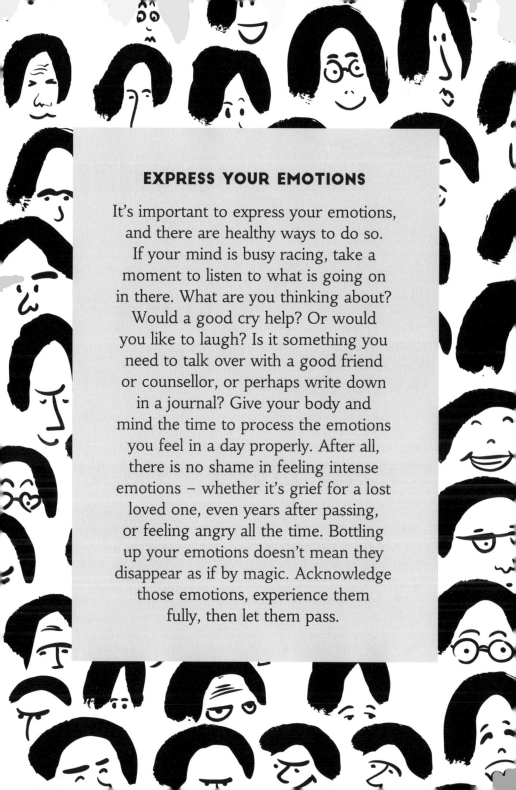

EXPRESS YOUR EMOTIONS

It's important to express your emotions, and there are healthy ways to do so. If your mind is busy racing, take a moment to listen to what is going on in there. What are you thinking about? Would a good cry help? Or would you like to laugh? Is it something you need to talk over with a good friend or counsellor, or perhaps write down in a journal? Give your body and mind the time to process the emotions you feel in a day properly. After all, there is no shame in feeling intense emotions – whether it's grief for a lost loved one, even years after passing, or feeling angry all the time. Bottling up your emotions doesn't mean they disappear as if by magic. Acknowledge those emotions, experience them fully, then let them pass.

Never assume that loud is strong

and

quiet is weak

SHOW YOUR MIND WHO'S BOSS

Switch it up a bit in your head. Your thoughts don't control you; it's the other way around. You are dominant. You are in charge. You control your thoughts. Tell your mind it's had its fun, but now you're going to be taking back control and setting a calmer, more positive route ahead.

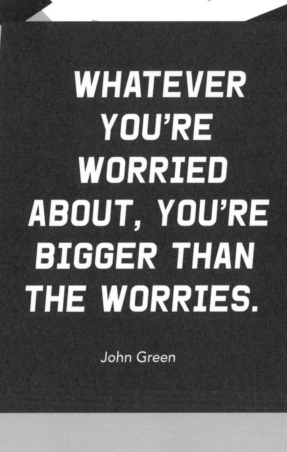

WHATEVER YOU'RE WORRIED ABOUT, YOU'RE BIGGER THAN THE WORRIES.

John Green

WOULD YOU SAY IT TO A FRIEND?

Practise realistic thinking. Notice when your thoughts are beginning to turn to the negative, or to self-criticisms, and put yourself in a friend or family member's shoes – what would you say to someone experiencing what you are right now? Would you say the thoughts in your head to them? If not, then why would you say them to yourself?

PEACE
AND
QUIET

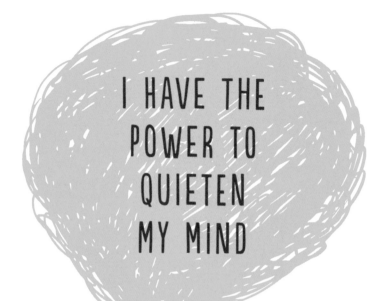

PEACE AND QUIET

Explore meditation. Meditation is
a well-established path to inner
peace, and an excellent way to re-
centre yourself when you're feeling
overwhelmed with everything modern
life has to throw at you. Find a class or
online video that focuses on calming
an overactive mind, and set aside the
time to try it seriously. Create a cosy
environment in your home to practise,
somewhere you feel safe and still
and will be uninterrupted. There are
several different strands of meditation,
which vary from those that advocate
completely silencing your inner voice
for the duration of the practice, to
those which encourage you to watch
your thoughts as they naturally come
and go, so experiment with a few to
find the style that works best for you.

CHECK IN WITH YOUR BODY

Another way to practise meditation is to perform a full-body scan. Lie somewhere comfortable, warm and quiet, where you will not be interrupted. Take your time and slowly start to 'check in' with your body, seeing how it feels. Start at the head, then work your way down the body, shifting your attention to each area in turn and acknowledging any aches or tension. Try to actively tense and then release each muscle in turn, and feel the sensation of gravity pressing you into the floor or mattress and taking the weight of your body. It is rare that we take the time to truly notice how every part of our body is feeling, but this can be a calming and meditative ritual that you can easily build into your daily life.

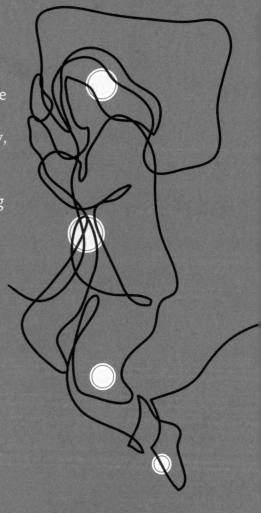

GET OUT
OF YOUR
HEAD

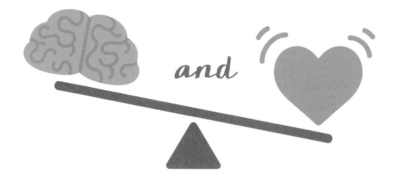

and

GET INTO
YOUR
HEART.

Think less, feel more.

Osho

CENTRE YOURSELF

Next time you feel your thoughts spiralling
out of control, take a big, deep breath
and breathe out, counting slowly to three.
Focus on your breath, and on the counting,
to bring your awareness to your body
and away from unproductive thought
patterns. This is one of the quickest and
easiest ways to interrupt a busy mind and
quickly calm it down. Alternatively, if
counting doesn't work for you, try focusing
intently on a picture of something you find
calming – it might be an empty beach,
or a calm pond – for a few seconds.

EMBRACE EMBRACES

Ask a friend or family member for
a hug! Hugging others releases a
'happy hormone' that relaxes you
and reinforces relationships, so not
only will you be reminding your
friend that they are loved by you, but
also you'll get a boost of happiness
and serenity out of the deal.

A QUIET MIND CAN HEAR INTUITION

OVER FEAR

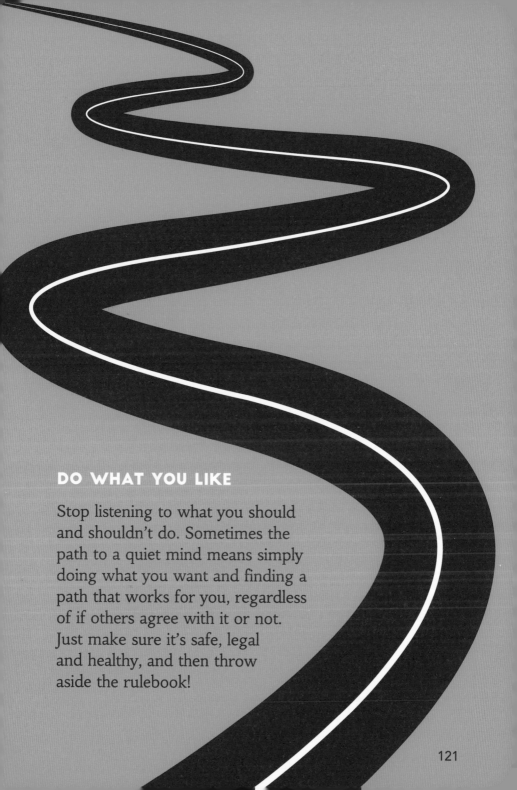

DO WHAT YOU LIKE

Stop listening to what you should
and shouldn't do. Sometimes the
path to a quiet mind means simply
doing what you want and finding a
path that works for you, regardless
of if others agree with it or not.
Just make sure it's safe, legal
and healthy, and then throw
aside the rulebook!

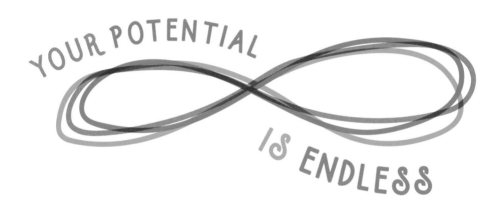

YOUR POTENTIAL IS ENDLESS

JUST LAUGH!

Book tickets to see your favourite comedian or watch some open-mic stand-up, put on a movie that makes you giggle or reminisce with a friend about all the things you used to get up to. Remind yourself that life isn't so bad and that there's a lot of silliness, fun and positivity in the world.

EXERCISE TO CLEAR YOUR MIND

Go for a jog, swim or bike ride several times a week. Nothing clears the mind better than a quick burst of activity and some fresh air. If you feel like you can't fit exercise into your day, do small switches instead, such as getting off the bus a stop early or cycling to work or the shops instead of driving.

STAY AFRAID, BUT DO IT ANYWAY.

Carrie Fisher

GET OUT AND GET MOVING!

Spend an afternoon going for a walk along the beach, or hiking in a nearby wood or to a local beauty spot. Enjoy looking for birds in the trees or the sky, for fish in rivers, lakes or the sea, and for any other wildlife you might spot on the way. Find a pretty rock or shell and keep it as a keepsake to decorate your home with, and to remind yourself of the pleasant, quiet time you had in the great outdoors. Admire your surroundings and take in the small details: the sound of birdsong, the fresh air and sunshine on your skin, the wind in your hair, the crunch of sand or gravel underfoot. Let these refresh you and re-energise you. Your mind will have time to think things through properly, and the activity will keep your body releasing positive hormones.

I feel within me
a peace above all
earthly dignities,
a still and quiet
conscience.

William Shakespeare

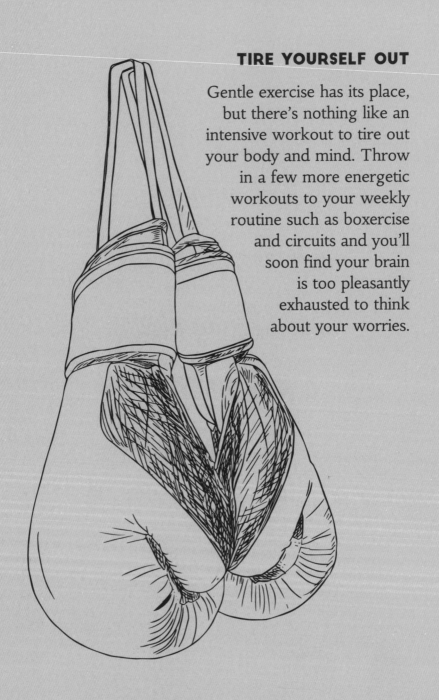

TIRE YOURSELF OUT

Gentle exercise has its place,
but there's nothing like an
intensive workout to tire out
your body and mind. Throw
in a few more energetic
workouts to your weekly
routine such as boxercise
and circuits and you'll
soon find your brain
is too pleasantly
exhausted to think
about your worries.

TRY YOGA

Yoga is a gentle form of exercise, but one which improves strength and flexibility and really helps stretch out your muscles, leaving you feeling peaceful and relaxed – the perfect exercise for an overactive mind. Look for classes nearby, or find online videos or DVDs that will get you practising some basic poses and sequences in the comfort of your own home.

DON'T BE AFRAID TO *flourish*

PRACTISE VISUALISATION

Picture somewhere that feels calm to you –
perhaps you are in a field, or relaxing on a boat
in a lake or floating on a cloud in a blue sky.
Visualise yourself taking hold of the thoughts
that plague you, putting them into a bubble and
then releasing it. Let the wind take it and watch it
float away, allowing the thoughts to vanish in the
distance and become insignificant. Tell yourself
those thoughts can't bother you anymore. Return
to this calm place of release whenever your mind
feels full of unhelpful thoughts, and know you
always have this safe space to go to, where all
negative thoughts are banished and you can relax.

DISTRACT YOUR MIND

When your mind is fixating on negative thoughts or starting to panic, here's a trick you can use wherever you are, in any situation, for a moment of instant distraction. Close your eyes and look to see what is actually there. It often isn't just completely black, but filled with other colours, and swirling patterns and shapes. Let your mind get lost in these hypnotic phenomena and shift your attention away from your busy thoughts.

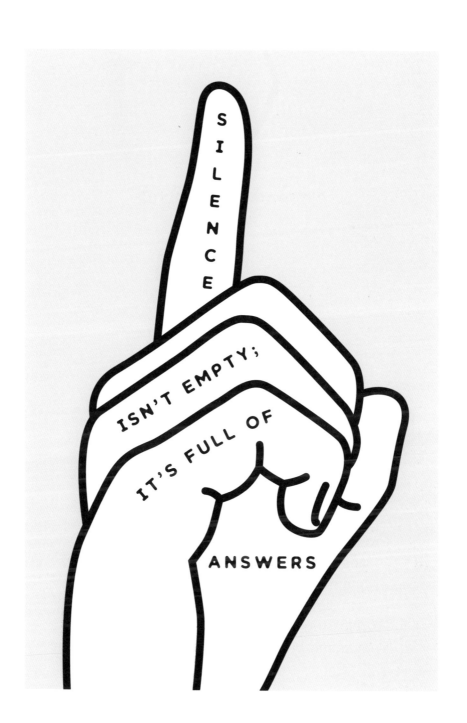

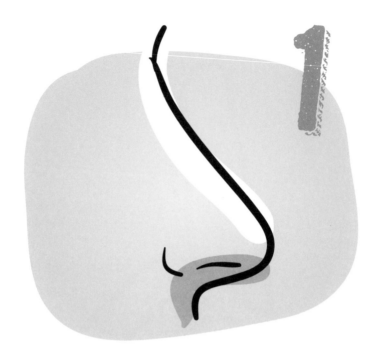

PRACTISE BREATHING TECHNIQUES

Alternate-nostril breathing takes our
minds' focus away from everything that's
going on in our daily lives. It also brings
our awareness to our body and fresh air
and oxygen to our lungs. Try pressing
one nostril gently closed and breathing
in slowly for a count of three, then
releasing that nostril, closing the other
side and breathing out on the first side

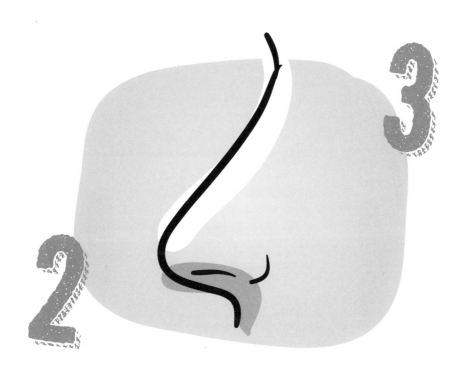

for a count of three. Pause briefly, then inhale through that same side slowly, swap nostrils and breathe out again. You can steadily increase the number of counts you inhale and exhale for, slowing your breathing right down. Repeat for several minutes every day, or whenever you need to bring your heart rate down.

The inspiration
you seek
is already
within you.
Be silent
and listen.

Rumi

BE AT PEACE WITH YOURSELF

LEARN TO LOVE YOURSELF

It's perfectly normal to look back at your past self and be critical, but try to forgive yourself for any perceived mistakes – accept yourself for who you were and who you are now. Everyone makes mistakes as they grow up – it is how we learn and develop as people. Learn to thank and love the past you for making you who you are today. Turn the things you consider your past weaknesses into strengths. For example, if teenage you couldn't manage time correctly, thank them for making that mistake for you: now you know the importance of it and can take the right steps in dealing with it. Acknowledge that you are the only person who can live your life. Give yourself kudos for making it to where you are now. Always remember that comparing yourself to others is futile: other people may have done things differently, but that does not always mean better. There is only one you – take the time to love the person you have become for all of your past experiences.

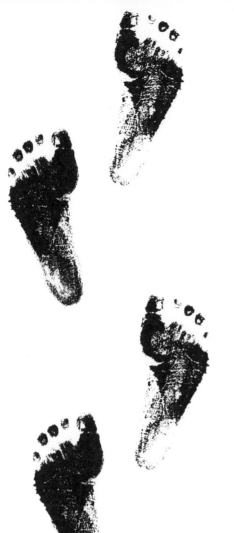

i will not let anyone walk through my mind with their dirty feet.

Mahatma Gandhi

LET THE PAST BE THE PAST

There is nothing you can do to turn back time, and the moments you linger on more often than not turn out to be insignificant when you look back on them. Learn from past experiences, but try not to dwell on things that aren't productive. Let the past be.

DEAL WITH
PERSISTENT THOUGHTS

If your mind keeps bringing up a
specific event or person, then think
about what might be unresolved.
Your subconscious mind might be
asking for closure or forgiveness,
so if you can take steps to alleviate
any bad feelings you're holding on
to, then take them. Maybe you feel
the need to apologise to someone
you didn't treat right, or get back
in touch with an old friend?

CARE ABOUT WHAT OTHERS THINK AND YOU WILL ALWAYS BE THEIR PRISONER.

Lao Tzu

YOU CAN'T GO BACK AND CHANGE THE BEGINNING, BUT YOU CAN START WHERE YOU ARE AND CHANGE THE ENDING.

C. S. Lewis

YOU ARE WORTHY

When you're worried it's easy to slip into a negative thought spiral, which often ends up with thinking that you aren't capable or worthy of something. Don't let these thoughts take over. You are deserving of love, happiness and success. Know that you are worthy and hold your head high.

YOU ARE DOING THINGS AT YOUR OWN PACE, AND THAT'S OK

LET IT GO

When we don't agree with something someone else says or believes, it's all too easy for our brains to go into overdrive trying to 'correct' them or get angry at their different way of thinking. Try to be more open and accepting of other people's beliefs. You don't need to agree with them, but unless other people's ideas physically affect you, you're only harming yourself by getting caught up in them. Let them believe what they want to, and give your mind permission to let go of the issue.

DO A GOOD DEED

Do something nice for someone else. Everyone is going through their own struggles, so if you can find a way to help someone else, you'll not only get the pleasant feeling of knowing you've done a good deed, but you might also make new contacts who you can turn to in your times of need.

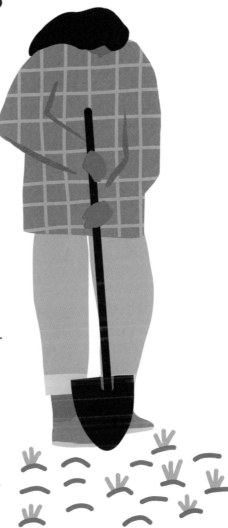

SAY 'THANK YOU' MORE

It's all too easy to simply go about our day without properly acknowledging those who help us through it. By being thankful and actively appreciating the good things in your day, you can get a long way in finding a more positive and relaxed outlook.

SEEK TO
BE STILL
WITH
OTHERS

MOST MEN LEAD LIVES OF QUIET DESPERATION, AND GO TO THE GRAVE WITH THE SONG STILL IN THEM.

Henry David Thoreau

SPEND TIME WITH YOUR FRIENDS AND FAMILY

An overly busy mind can often be stilled and quietened by the company of others. Surround yourself with those who love you and wish nothing but the best for you, and you may find your mind naturally calms down to focus on the people you love. If it doesn't, try opening up to them about what's plaguing you. You may find that they have

good advice to offer or ideas you hadn't thought of. Sharing your worries with other people can allow you to focus on solving problems that keep running through your mind, or help you to see things in a new light, giving you perspective. A healthy friendship or family relationship should include unconditional love, support and encouragement, and the company of those who cherish you should bring your mind some much-needed peace.

MEDICAL ADVICE

If you have reached the end of this book and tried the ideas and techniques within, but still feel like you are unable to achieve a quieter mind, it may be the right time to seek professional help. Book an appointment with your GP to see what they recommend. Remember to tell them everything; there is nothing they haven't heard before. The more honest you are and the more detail you give, the more you give your GP a better chance of finding a treatment that will work for you.

IMAGE CREDITS